In the Herald of Improbable Misfortunes

In the Herald of Improbable Misfortunes

Robert Campbell

Etchings Press
Indianapolis, Indiana

Copyright © 2018 Robert Campbell

This publication is made possible by funding provided by the Shaheen College of Arts and Sciences and the English Department of the University of Indianapolis. Special thanks to IngramSpark and to those students who judged, edited, designed, and published this chapbook: Rochelle Bauer and Savannah Harris.

University *of*
INDIANAPOLIS

Published by Etchings Press
1400 E. Hanna Ave
Indianapolis, Indiana 46227
All rights reserved.

blogs.uindy.edu/etchings/
www.uindy.edu/cas/english

Printed by Ingram Spark
www.ingramspark.com

Printed in the United States of America

ISBN-13: 978-0-9903475-8-3
23 22 21 20 19 18   2 3 4
Second Printing, 2019

Colophon
Body text: Optima
Cover title, titles, and poem titles: Trattatello
Graphics: "The Moon," 17th century Tarocco di Besancon
by J. B. Benois

Many thanks to the editors of the publications where these poems have appeared, sometimes in previous forms:

The Adroit Journal: "Elegy for the Oft-Fabled Stepchild" and "You Are Thinking of the Tool-Shed, Jet-Black Hornets"

The Collagist: "Jesus for Lobsters"

Columbia Poetry Review: "Percussion in the Valley of Dry Bones"

DIALOGIST: "Movie in Which We Are Drowning"

Los Angeles Review: "Dear Stranger, I Remember You Before the Collision"

Nashville Review: "Dream in Which My Body Is a Knife"

Radar Poetry: "Dream in Which I Am Farming Loneliness"

River Styx: "Arrhythmia"

Slice Magazine: "Theater of Elsewhere"

Tinderbox Poetry Journal: "Important Facts About Dreaming"

Zone 3: "In the Herald of Improbable Misfortunes"

Table of Contents

In the Herald of Improbable Misfortunes 1

Important Facts About Dreaming 2

Dear Stranger, I Remember You Before the Collision 4

Dream in Which My Body Is a Knife 6

Arrhythmia 7

Jesus for Lobsters 9

You Are Thinking of the Tool-Shed, Jet-Black Hornets 10

Movie in Which We Are Drowning 12

Elegy for the Oft-Fabled Stepchild 13

The Lamp Factory Is Dreaming 15

Percussion in the Valley of Dry Bones 16

Dream in Which I Am Farming Loneliness 17

Theater of Elsewhere 18

For Keagan

In the Herald of Improbable Misfortunes

Trouble the reader. Both of which
matter. A matter unsettled. A grip

arthritic. Here is an article, pointed
and angled. A2: *Man Attacked by Naked*

Face-eater. A4: *Mother Feeds Children
to Wild Bear*. They matter dearly,

these events of mention. Let's
start over. Here is a little mention

in the paper. B6. We know the reader
is plagued and wearied, ink-heeled

by these endearing matters. B9: Today,
in Nova Scotia, a twelve-ton statue

hewn from salt and sedimentary rock—
a loose depiction of Prometheus-as-

dentist—embarked for purgatory, and fell
into the sea. Let the matter be settled.

We are pleased to report that the readership
remains settled. Inform the readership. Settle

in. This, our mention. We wept over it,
and it learned to swim. Amoebic, it floated

towards the light, gesturing emergency,
a matter unsettling. Fear not, reader. This

is our duty: to inform you of developments
and departures, of every last unhappening.

Important Facts About Dreaming

I.

Five minutes: that's the average stretch
for which the pillowed psychonaut
will wander. Such excursions
are chiseled on stone tablets
dated 3100 B.C. This, the act
of *condensation*, precipitory—
the beads of water on our foreheads
a rain that has always, already come.

II.

We *go* to sleep. We vacation there,
swaddling ourselves along its dunes
to hear our blood thrash back and forth,
lapping at our little boat. Note how,
in the Upanishads, there are two kinds
of dreams: the mere expression of craving—
I need I fear I want I strain I covet—
and the utter evacuation of the body.

III.

In terms of both dream length and frequency,
the order goes like this: possums, horses,
us—all swept up in the ghosting current
of memorized recombinants, backwater,
all of us dangled in the warm, black air.

IV.

Freud said:

Subconscious Oraculum Womb Repression Phallus etc.

Possum says:

Hang, inebriate. Be bright
mathematics. Build
night cities. Invert
firmament. Unleash
stray dogs of orchestra.

V.

Time, after all, can be said to dilate
inside the body, the parietal lobe
flexing its muscle, racing its oil
like chemical horses, seeking music.

Dear Stranger, I Remember You Before the Collision

I.

When I was a deer, I thought like a deer. I reasoned
like a deer, gazing at you across the fog-thick highway,
pearl-eyed, watching you sleep in your crumpled Volvo.

Like a deer, I bent to chew and think. And when, at last,
I became a man, I gave up deerish ways. I shook my antlers
and pulled up my pants. I stumbled into the fluorescent

office lights, the tick-tock of keyboards. My hooves are clean
and black, and in your mind, I am walking towards you in some
tiled hallway. I am going to utter something to you now,

something animal and so true, some secret between
passengers, clearer to your own cells than to you:
we have two bodies, two anatomies of weakness.

II.

When I was among the wind and the grass, I spoke
like a reed, I dreamed seed dreams. Come closer, you heartache,
you dizzied little lonesome. There was a god who lived

in a thorny bush, beside the broken-down train station
and up the hill. And he climbed up into the rust-eaten cars
and sang his thorny bush songs. And the ghosts of the trains

would grind and shake up dust, and their whistles drifted
cobwebs in the dark. I am not a deer, dear reader, and I am not
a man. This is the echo in which we are sitting now, just

the two of us. Can you see my antlers? Can you see
the bone-white thorny bush of my antlers, snagging corners
of the shadow of this room? When I was a deer, I ate men's hearts

and had three faces. I shined in three directions like a star.
When I became a man, I bent and curled and shrank. Dear
passenger, I folded into myself, trading miles for feet.

III.

I know you wonder about the crashed Volvo. I know
you worry so. You want a story you can stomach, stranger,
no ghosts in the hills, no gods in trains. We wander, though,

and we winter this way—in so many directions. We poke,
we prod into the chilling air. We harden our stories into crowns
and wear them on our heads, massive and pointed, clashing

and stumbling, clumsy gods. When I was a deer, I would stroll
through that old train station, and each car had a human name,
each in its place, alphabetical: *Aaron, Adele, Adrian, Amos,*

Amy, Anthony, Arthur, and so on. Little sing-song steps.
Listen hard; you know this song. Let us tearfully go down
into that valley, graceful and deerish, dreaming deer dreams.

Dream in Which My Body Is a Knife

I grind my teeth on a coarse, black stone.
Sharp-shouldered, I crave a stranger

to cover me on cold nights like a sheath.
When you look into my body, you can see

your own reflection there. Hunter, tuck me
into your boot like a little note. Dash me

against gravel to spark fire. Drag me
along the sides of pickup trucks. Watch

as I divide pretense: anyone I look at splits into
two people. I have no someone. The woods

have no someone. I want to slide into the soft
dirt. I want to fall against the rocks and sing.

Arrhythmia

Between seasons, the reddest muscle
bleats inside its pale stone cage, trots
in circles. Where in the trembling world

do music and breathing come from?
Wet pulse. Blood loaf. Animal hive
wired with *rat-tat-tat*. All of our houses

have asked themselves the difference
between inside, outside, which type of nothing
is harder to swallow. My house has red shutters

and mutters at night. The muscle
is unnerved by windows   and by mirrors.
It shivers to think of itself, poised

on rattling sticks for legs, fragile as
a phrase of zither music—and as temporary.
In my basement, you can hear the water rush

from one pipe to another, though it sounds more
like old women shushing a child
or some poor farm animal crying out

as it's throttled and dragged to a shed
with one memorable purpose.
Shear you, leave you cold. Isn't that the season,

the hour, the inch that flushes us pale—a crack
in an otherwise airtight   fortress?
This red keep, knot of pitch dark tunnels,

labyrinthine and locked up tight. My house
has a well-laid roof. My house has a very
solid   foundation. Open the window,

and the room howls its lungs out—that's called
negative pressure, in which the home's membrane
pulls in too much (and that, too, has a song).

Jesus for Lobsters

Say there are fifteen holy beatitudes for lobsters.
Pretend with me. *Blessed are the spiny ones,*

for their hearts shall be smoothest. That's number
twelve. *Blessed are they who perish beneath*

the huddled mass of weaponry, for they shall see
the lobster god. That's number seven. What do

we know about lobsters, really, beneath armored
shadow-anatomies, lumbering about

in the supermarket aquarium, scuttling silently,
pincers bound? What do we know about the god

that lobsters pray to? About what angels carry
such barbed artilleries of red, and to what kingdoms,

by what covenant? We don't know anything
about the lobster Jesus, his calcite throne

of antler reef. I think he would be wise and hard, hard
to love, his claws and antennae red, infernal almost,

his sayings secret and severe. Lobster Jesus
is neither kind nor personal. He isn't going

to save you. No, the men are coming with their pot,
their forks, their metal tongs to crack your carapace

in two. They want your treasures to be cheap,
yielding, the shell of you strewn across a table.

You Are Thinking of the Tool Shed, Jet-black Hornets

Rust-eaten shears. Oak stool. Floorboards
worn and cracked. You are thinking of that shed

full of hornets. It leaned its stack beside the creek,
ornery and bent. In cool Octobers, dreadful

ornaments grew in its corners, story-fed, born
through wood-grit, horned and humming. Who

would get the wood there, fetch the rake, wet
from the leaking rain? Stray cats collided. Your

youngest uncle's Marlboro hack. His hair
was red, not jet-black. The hornets burrowed,

then rose above the stacks of firewood, unfurling
like a cloud. Burn it. Scuttling back, blue-black

almost, purring on the pile of boards. This
is the red welt on your leg. Mourn it almost,

the stinging hive-bed. Even if you can't recall
what home-grown beans taste like, you'll have

the scar still when you call to explain again
why you aren't married—or saved—or coming

for Thanksgiving. Keep it simple, kid. Shut
the tool shed door, let the latch turn, spurn it

like a fool, go off angrier than the roaring
branches in the storm, its sack of cold wind,

its scorn, its mules unfed. Even if you could return,
where would you look for your cracked palms,

your old southern drawl? What would you bet
against the coming clouds? Would you even bet?

Movie in Which We Are Drowning

Like a pot of water cooling on the stove,
we eventually reach room temperature. Who knows
what for. The liver grows heavy with holes

grown heavy with pebbles, malignant. Pinhole
camera, little black looking box. The skin
slips against the weight of the body like a tent

in hard rainfall. None of this is remarkable,
not really, not when you consider the rate
at which steam rises, its molecules seeking out

the cold. Everything wants to be condensed. Focus
a memory, and it shrinks for the aperture. The body
shrivels, laughable. Sad, but not remarkable.

Imagine life as a silent film, true black and white, black
being utter blackness, white like fog in headlights.
Sickly white—a white sink under fluorescent

bulbs. Noisy, buzzing white. The viewer is blind;
he sits too close to the screen. *Click-click*
goes the film reel, elliptical. Sad, but not remarkable.

Imagine the water outside has risen, a constant rain
is falling, the leak has sprung. The big one. The floor
of the theater looks solid enough, then rises to meet

the skirts of female viewers, its surface forgiving
as a river. The floor is a river floating popcorn. Here
is your boat; it is reddish brown, red like a liver.

Elegy for the Oft-Fabled Stepchild

Before the boy will appear to you,
you must tell the whole story again.
Hear him descend the crooked stair.

Picture him pressed and tucked beside
the kitchen sink, reaching for the fruit bowl.
Picture the room unfathomable: clock

of ivory, red floor, antique oak table,
and his head rolling off of its trunk,
clicking open like a lock, in its seventy-

eighth month, in which she blanched
his pieces into nothings as spilled flour
haunted the window, the table. This

is the yard untillable. The ground bloomed
fathoms of stinging weed-flowers. What
if all mothers kept trunks, which they

must hide? What if all fathers devoured
their young? What if we could sing
to children through holes in the dirt like

precious stones? You will not find him—
not in a thousand years will you mine
him from the fallow silt. Listen—

close your eyes. He's gone as breath,
never where you left him, disentangled
from the family tree. And you, teller,

how you wish he would be still. There
goes the oft-fabled stepchild now,
mind wandering, directionless as pollen,

top lopped off like a dandelion, tumbled
under and thither, rolling among the crab-
apples, past the blue-feathered hills.

The Lamp Factory Is Dreaming

of its blue fumes and *objets d'art*.
Wheels in motion, it cranks its plumes

into the atmosphere, gray and wet, gray
as a whale's heart. The lamp factory

beside the railroad tracks is dreaming,
and all the trees along the tracks swoon

towards its dream-wattage. Men march in
and out of it in white coats. The mid-winter

elms are black with rain. In the dark hours
of morning, the parking lot shines, slick

with yellow light. Scuttle of concrete
and rubber boots. The factory dreams

and breathes into the city, empties itself
by iron pipe, by gear and grind, cut

and pressed, white-hot, dunked until
it screams shrill steam, ready at last

to illuminate strangers' living rooms
in hours of darkness, ready to give

itself to the neatly folded box of white,
to be carted off to some new asphalt life.

Percussion in the Valley of Dry Bones

The Lord set me in the middle of a valley. It was full of bones.
I will open your graves and declare important things, He said.

The Lord grabbed two hills and broke the crust of the earth.
I will make various pronouncements on your heads, He said.

The Lord mused, rubbing the chin of his golden countenance.
My people will sing unto me, and I will tap my feet in time.

The Lord unpeeled some stratosphere and rolled a cigarette.
Afterward, I would like a very nice reception with limoncello.

The Lord passed his hand over the bones; they began to drop
a syncopated beat. *I will dangle the skeletons of men from strings*

while playing Beastie Boys songs on keytar. The Lord breathed,
and fog and strobe lights issued from each skull. *I will break-dance*

for my people. I will pop and lock with glory. The Lord gyrated
on his chariot, and it did thunder and lightning; the firmament

hissed with steam. *My people will pay one hundred and fifty bucks
to see me lowered onto a stage wearing nothing but pink sequins*

and fingerless gloves, received into a throng of dancers. The Lord
grew indecipherable. He beat-boxed for twenty minutes straight,

and the heavenly host did twist and shake. *I will perform my final
number with pyrotechnics and with smoke.* The sky grew dark,

a great yawning in the abyss. The skeletons hummed. The Lord
flicked ash into the sea, and when I opened my mouth to speak,

he stuck his lit cigarette therein. It seared my tongue. And then
I returned to Jerusalem, no wiser, but blind and full of music.

Dream in Which I Am Farming Loneliness

I can plow the mile-long grooves of this season
with a boot-knife plucked from a scarecrow's back.

Ten birds punctuate a wire. I drag my instrument
in furrows—I am pulling the field's lines

toward me, toward ten perches, ten not-you's.
The dirt is fat with rain, heavy and black,

moist root-bits and manure. If you opened
your mouth in this season, a blue jay might wrestle

itself loose. There's no end to these hard digs.
And the mock-passenger, screwed to a post,

the stitch-smiled dummy with your lips, says:
Hang up, October. Hang up, birds. Hang up, you.

Theater of Elsewhere

Think of it—imagine yourself
among the Spanish oaks on this

thick, humid night. A chill
finds you. An eerie glow

in the fog. Ferns billow at
your bare feet. Here lies that

dead gesture, once a comfort.
You've never felt so awake.

Dreams are not merely our pretty
theater of elsewhere—there's

a wildness unsanctioned. All of what
you can't contain is there: mess

of weeds and moss, fireflies
cajoling above the blue-black pool,

and shadows, too. You know
this place. The chemical agent

that illumines firefox is called
luciferase. What makes

remembering burn? Wanderer,
think of all the ones who plodded

these same paths never to return.
(Various versions: drowned, hunted,
poisoned by bitter nightshade
berries.) How woods shine

in the right light. How carefully
our weak and idle themes carry

their little lights between the trees.

Etchings Press

Etchings Press is a student-run publisher at the University of Indianapolis. Each year, student editors choose the Whirling Prize, a post-publication award, in the fall and coordinate a publication contest for one poetry chapbook, one prose chapbook, and one novella in the spring. For more information, please visit etchings.uindy.edu.

Previous winners and publications

Poetry
2019: *As Lovers Always Do* by Marne Wilson
2018: *In the Herald of Improbable Misfortunes*
        by Robert Campbell
2017: *Uncle Harold's Maxwell House Haggadah* by Danny Caine
2016: *Some Animals* by Kelli Allen
2015: *Velocity of Slugs* by Joey Connelly
2014: *Action at a Distance* by Christopher Petruccelli

Prose
2019: *Dissenting Opinion from the Committee for the Beatitudes*
        by Marc J. Sheehan (fiction)
2018: *The Forsaken* by Chad V. Broughman (fiction)
2017: *Unravelings* by Sarah Cheshire (memoir)
2016: *Pathetic* by Shannon McLeod (essays)
2015: *Ologies* by Chelsea Biondolillo (essays)
2014: *Static: Stories* by Frederick Pelzer (fiction)

Novella
2019: *Savonne, Not Vonny* by Robin Lee Lovelace
2018: *Edge of the Known Bus Line* by James R. Gapinski
2017: *The Denialist's Almanac of American Plague and*
        Pestilence by Christopher Mohar
2016: *Followers* by Adam Fleming Petty

Robert Campbell's poetry and criticism have appeared in *Tupelo Quarterly, The Collagist, Columbia Poetry Review, River Styx, Ninth Letter, Asheville Poetry Review, Tinderbox Poetry Journal, Sundog Lit, Zone 3, The Adroit Journal,* and many other journals. Twice nominated for the Pushcart Prize, short-listed for the 2015 Black Warrior Review Poetry Contest, third place winner of the 2013 River Styx International Poetry Contest, and previous winner of the Flo Gault Poetry Prize through Sarabande Books, Robert holds an MFA in Poetry from Murray State University and an MS in Library Science from the University of Kentucky. He lives with his partner and animals on a winding country road in the bluegrass region of Kentucky.

www.ingramcontent.com/pod-product-compliance
Lightning Source LLC
Chambersburg PA
CBHW070443010526
44118CB00014B/2168